The Origins of British Photography

Introduction by Mark Haworth-Booth

Thames and Hudson

Biographies translated from the French by Ruth Sharman

First published in Great Britain in 1991 by
Thames and Hudson Ltd, London
Originally published in France by the Centre National de la Photographie
Copyright © 1988 by Centre National de la Photographie, Paris

Printed and bound in Italy

The Origins of
British Photography

1

Short loan
770.92
Acc 4010

A GOLDEN AGE OF PHOTOGRAPHY

When did photography begin in Britain? Was it one of the earliest inventions of the reign of Queen Victoria, who ascended the throne in 1837? Or a last effort of the reign of William IV – in which case we might regard it as belonging to the Age of Reform – or was it a characteristic product of the age of Romanticism and Revolution? It would be the last of these if we took as the starting point of photography in Britain the experiments of Thomas Wedgwood and Sir Humphry Davy in 1801-2. The two scientists were able to make images with light on light-sensitive paper and leather but not able to fix them. Their epoch-making achievement did not, in the event, make an epoch: perhaps somewhere there still exist today blank pieces of paper which once bore traces of photographic imagery seen, briefly, by Wedgwood, Davy and their friends. The story is well known of how the brilliant young scientist William Henry Fox Talbot (1800-1877), during his honeymoon on Lake Como in 1833, practised drawing with the aid of a camera lucida. This optical instrument operated by throwing an image of a scene on to a sheet of paper upon which a draughtsman – even an inexperienced one – could then trace the outlines of this scene, or landscape. Talbot became dissatisfied by his pencil sketches and began to ponder how the actual image from the lens of the camera lucida could be caught in all its tonal, as well as linear, variety. His speculations pursued a path already explored by his English predecessors – Wedgwood and Davy – and, of course, the great French pioneers Niepce and Daguerre. Talbot's expertise in chemistry and optics enabled him to realize his desire to trap the 'inimitable beauty of the pictures of Nature's painting', these 'fairy pictures, creations of a moment'. He began experimenting with salt and silver nitrate and by 1835 he had managed to stabilize camera lucida images on light-sensitive paper. Spurred on by the progress of Daguerre, Talbot brought his efforts to the attention of the scientific community – and to the larger public realm – in demonstrations and communications in January and February 1839. He perfected his 'Calotype' process in 1841 and published *The Pencil of Nature* in a series of six instalments beginning in June 1844. These little pamphlets contained introductory texts by Talbot and original calotype photographs.

It is important to decide when photography was invented in order to assess what matrix of cultural history, including political history, the invention is part of and to which it most intimately belongs. As we shall see, the medium of photography became a paradigm of two qualities which sometimes seem opposed: in the 1850s photography was asserted to be a pristine method of creating fresh images of nature 'painted by Nature herself' (in a standard phrase of the time) and also a method of routine social interaction, a method of propagating (in Lady Eastlake's splendid phrase of 1857) 'cheap, prompt and correct facts'. The two opposite approaches to the meaning of photography could perhaps be united into a higher whole if we recall that the almost successful experiments of about 1800 are close in date to the revolutionary period. Many of those who have lived by photography in the last 150 years have found its special attention to lie in its combination of a pristine directness of method and an apparently universal breadth of social use. Such an underlying ideology, or one like it, will have an influence on the way the illustrations in this volume are appreciated and understood.

The circle of Henry Fox Talbot produced many of the most distinguished calotypists. Despite its inventor's attempts to popularize it, Talbot's paper photographs (as opposed to the silvered plates of the daguerreotype) were known to only a limited public during the 1840s. Among the most impressive practitioners were Talbot himself, his acquaintance the Reverend Calvert Richard Jones (1804-1877) and his kinsman John Dillwyn Llewelyn (1810-1882). The prints they made in the 1840s have in an astonishing number of cases survived in immaculate physical condition, with no apparent deterioration at all. Many prints look so fine that, were their provenance not absolutely secure, they would be under suspicion as masterpieces of the faker's art. In contrast to the invention of Daguerre, Talbot's contribution was to invent the negative/positive process, giving photography the possibility of industrialization and unlimited replication. *The Pencil of Nature* was designed by Talbot to illustrate the potential of the process – as a method of taking picturesque views after the manner of Dutch paintings of the seventeenth century, copying old texts, sculptures or paintings, preserving the likeness of historical buildings, making an inventory of books or china, making studies of trees and parkland. He set up a 'Photographic Establishment' at Reading (a town between his estate at Lacock Abbey in Wiltshire and London) but his efforts were launched on a world as yet unprepared for the new medium. Members of Talbot's circle, like Jones and Llewelyn, made memorable and poetic images with the calotype process. Their work was artistic, inspiring and educational – and perhaps from it they hoped to realize a suitable financial return.

Apart from Talbot's own establishment, the most ambitious and well-organized calotype undertaking in Britain was that of the Hill and Adamson partnership in Edinburgh. The partnership is pleasingly symbolic of the early phase of the medium, being composed of a chemist – Robert Adamson (1821-1848) and a painter – David Octavius Hill (1802-1870). Their studio is a prototype of the fashionable portrait studio of later years. They were able to pose their subjects in a space hung with rare stuffs, in the manner of portrait paintings by Sir Henry Raeburn and others, and to reflect sunlight on to the subjects' faces by the use of mirrors. They brought an artfulness, but also a genuine sense of graphic distinction and grandeur, to their portraits. They photographed those in Edinburgh's social 'swim', and they photographed the ministers and professors of the Church of Scotland who seceded from the church by signing the momentous Act of Separation and Deed of Demission in 1843. These men of conscience, together with a cast of artists, soldiers, fishermen and -women, occupy the impressive chiaroscuro of calotypes by Hill and Adamson. The first art-historical account of their work was by the Vienna-trained Heinrich Schwartz. His monograph *David Octavius Hill: Master of Photography* appeared in English in 1932. Writing at the time when the harsh conventions of

Neue Sachlichkeit style were becoming dominant in advanced portraiture in Central Europe, Schwartz noted a brilliant subtlety in the calotype portraits and suggested that the form of engraving known as mezzotint might have influenced Hill's lighting effects. Schwartz's remarks are still among the best on calotype, especially when he writes of the portraits with these characteristic ingredients: 'black lace gloves cover fine, intellectual hands; lace collars of dazzling white are spread over black silk, or frame a shadowed countenance; a gossamer lace nestles into the lines and folds of a sharp crinoline'. The partnership, like Talbot, offered views of landscape and architecture, genre scenes and cityscapes, working with inspiration and energy rather than notable financial reward. The most public, and the commercially dominant, version of photography during the 1840s was the portrait daguerreotype. The experience of being photographed was one of the new topicalities of the decade. The Irish novelist Maria Edgeworth left a vivid account in a letter: 'It is a wonderful mysterious operation. You are taken from one room into another up stairs and down and you see various people whispering and hear them in neighbouring passages and rooms unseen and the whole apparatus and stool on a high platform under a glass dome casting a snapdragon blue light making all look like spectres and the men in black gliding about . . . ' (*Letters from England, 1813-44*, ed. Christine Colvin, 1971, pp. 593-94).

A 'quantum leap' occurred in the development of photography in 1851. The major reason for this was the Great Exhibition held in London in that year and housed in that great symbol of new engineering and functional proto-modern architecture, the Crystal Palace. Here photographs from France, Britain and the United States competed for medals of merit and were admired by huge audiences. Suddenly the medium became credible as a method of making artistic pictures as well as making a living. A whole new group of individuals moved into the medium, or – as in the case of Benjamin Brecknell Turner (1815-1894), who was already photographing in 1849, suddenly heightened their ambitions. In addition to the great international spectacle offered by the photographic exhibits at the Crystal Palace, there were two key innovations. Frederick Scott Archer, an English sculptor and inventor, introduced his collodion-on-glass methods for negatives (1851). The previous year, L.D. Blanquart-Evrard introduced the albumen-coated papers which dominated production of positive prints until the last years of the century. Glass negatives cut exposure times and dramatically sharpened *The Pencil of Nature*. Glossy, albumen-coated papers gave new incisiveness and brilliance to positive proofs. The technical gains made possible new subjects and new approaches taken up by new practitioners and exhibition-scale prints became a feature of the scene. The first purely photographic exhibition ever mounted was held in 1852 under the auspices of the Society of Arts in London. From then on exhibitions implied a rapport, sometimes a competitively edged rapport, between photography and older and related media like painting in watercolours and printing from metal plates or stone. The 1850s saw a period of great inventiveness, and ambition, during which photography adapted the forms and ideas of earlier media and also challenged the commercial supremacy in the mass market of engravings and lithographs. A great deal of energy was also expended on ways of making a new photographically derived printing process so that the qualities of the new medium could be harnessed at once to the drive for a mass market.

Principal actors in the period of innovation in the 1850s were Roger Fenton (1819-1869), who took a leading role in founding The Photographic Society of London (which later became The Royal Photographic Society) in 1853, Dr Hugh Diamond (1808-1886), Philip Henry Delamotte (1821-1889), Robert Howlett (1831-1858) and Francis Bedford (1816-1894). All of these masters were touched in some way by the Great Exhibition. They all turned the new mechanical eye of photography on to the canonical subjects of the watercolour painting tradition. Their landscape photographs tested the new technology against traditional ideas of composition and tonality. Their experiments often included sheets of water in the foreground of their pictures, reflecting church or village beyond. Publications in the 1850s sometimes quote, opposite such photographs, lines of poetry based on William Wordsworth's notion of the mind, the creative imagination and nature. To some degree, perhaps quite consciously and deliberately, photographers of the time adopted a Wordsworthian, romantic, attitude to their medium. The sensitive photographic plate became a symbol or metaphor of the attentive mind, sensitized to the direct impressions of nature. Thus, the supposedly conservative nature of photographic imagery during this decade (much more concerned with the Picturesque tradition than with the Railway Age) may have been caused by its preoccupation with important philosophical notions. However, the pioneer photographers of the 1850s included those who, like Francis Bedford, would become effectively organized commercial producers of topographical imagery which ousted previous print forms. Bedford's landscapes became stock prints sold by country stationers for the albums of visitors and tourists.

During the 1860s Bedford, and other successful professional topographers, were overshadowed by the grand artistic, and entrepreneurial, achievements of Francis Frith (1822-1898). Frith made enormous and magnificent negatives of the Egyptian pyramids. He published albumen prints from these in book form in about 1860 as *Egypt, Sinai and Palestine*. The albumen prints were toned in gold chloride, a practice which both enhanced their tonal richness and protected them against fading. The prints remain monumental in scale and heroic in execution. It is most important to remember, when viewing photographs from the nineteenth century, that materials were often hand-made, or selected according to a practitioner's own procedures, and that development of the negative and printing (by sunlight, for much of the period) were done by close inspection. The craft, and artistic/interpretive, skills involved were high. There is no rising graph in aesthetic quality in photography. There is certainly an observable increase in convenience, but that is a different matter. Frith's 1860 photographs of the pyramids remain, I suspect, the best.

Frith's return from his first Egyptian trip (1856) was, significantly, greeted with acclaim by his fellow photographers. Frith was, perhaps, regarded as one who had extended the frontiers of photography. He had conquered – under the most extreme conditions, in which his collodion had actually simmered in the dark tent – a new world for photography (and, chauvinistically, of course for *British* photography). Photography spread across the terrains of ancient civilizations, bringing authentic documents of antiquity, and it spread – following the extraordinary expansion of the British Empire in these decades – across much of the globe. Frith's return to a hero's welcome in London indicates his importance in the battle of photography with its older commercial rivals (like lithography), in demonstrating its ability to present (and preserve) the great monuments of the world, and (perhaps) in symbolizing its purposeful annexation of exotic lands for the service of the commercial/political Empire, the Pax Britannica. Frank Mason Good (active 1860s-1880s) worked in a manner close to that of Bedford – who also made extensive views in the Mediterranean lands in 1862 – and contributed to Frith's photographic publishing business. This itself became an empire, procuring topographical views from many parts of the world and publishing them as albumen prints at the headquarters in Reigate, Surrey.

Photography successfully defined itself as a commercial entity during the 1850s and 1860s. It continued to seek an aesthetic identity in the same years. Fenton himself, like his great French equivalent Gustave Le Gray, pioneered many forms of photography: architectural, landscape, the narrative tableau, costume tableau (using clothing and other props from the Near East), the flower and fruit piece, cloudscape, semi-nude model, cityscape. More obviously painterly strategies were attempted by Oscar G. Rejlander (1813-1875), a Swedish painter and lithographer who emigrated to England and took up photography in 1853, and Henry Peach Robinson (1830-1901). Both men exhibited ambitious tableaux – figure compositions made by combining separately exposed negatives into one grand composition. The style was derived either from recent paintings distantly based on Raphael, or on the efforts of the Pre-Raphaelite school of painting (notably John Everett Millais). The results provoked criticism, debate, some purchases and some acclaim, but do not appear to have been taken at all seriously outside the photographic world. The really revolutionary aspects of photography were already making their way into painting at a more profound level – not as considered studio photographs but as instantaneous stereoscopic images of crowded city streets. However, the pioneer art photographers of the 1850s – like Rejlander and

Robinson – opened the way for more stylish and, in at least one case, more commercially successful art photographers in the 1860s. Most notable of the amateurs of the 1860s are Clementina, Viscountess Hawarden (no fewer than 775 prints by whom were later given to the Victoria and Albert Museum) and Julia Margaret Cameron. Lady Hawarden (1822-1865) was much admired by Rejlander, who may have instructed her at the beginning of her career. She worked with great speed, evidently, in her brief but productive career. Only now is the complexity of her work, which consists mainly of figure studies or tableaux involving her children, mainly photographed in South Kensington, London, beginning to receive careful study. However, her achievement was recognized in her lifetime by her peers, amateur and professional. Julia Margaret Cameron (1815-1879) is a most interesting example of the way photography developed after 1862. That year is in some ways decisive. If 1851 changed the climate of opinion about photography in Britain, encouraging a new group of talented individuals to experiment with the medium as amateurs and professionals (or a mixture of both), 1862 spelled the end of that particular phase and the triumph of photography as an industry. Roger Fenton and other heroes depart the medium in 1862 – but Francis Frith & Co. develops into an organization with world-wide interests. The practice of photography began to polarize. The age of the avowedly amateur began, coincidentally, with an entry by the newly formed Amateur Photographic Association at the International Exhibition held in London in 1862. Julia Margaret Cameron's work separates itself off from routine commercial portraiture by decisively using optical distortions for artistic ends. The enormous volume of prints by her which survive from the 1860s suggests that she met with considerable commercial, as well as critical, success. Again, the seriousness of her enterprise, particularly her inventiveness as a composer of religious subjects, has been accorded close study only in recent years.

Lady Eastlake, wife of the Director of The National Gallery, Sir Charles Eastlake, wrote of photography in 1857 as 'a household word and a household want, used alike by love, business and justice'. Photography grew to be part of social life during the years in which Dickens's novels regularly reached their wide and enthusiastic audience. The photographic elements in Dickens's prose style, and his interest in the vision and attributes of the detective, which in turn exhibit in his novels decidedly photographic qualities, are part of any wider appreciation of the role played by the medium in nineteenth-century English society. They can only be mentioned in passing here. Analysis of city life could not be – for technical reasons – a priority for photography in the nineteenth century. This graphic illustration was better achieved by the artists who made 'lightning sketches' for wood-engraved illustrations in periodicals. Photography only claimed this territory at the end of the century when small, inconspicuous hand-cameras, and quite quick (gelatin dry) plates – plus the beginnings of the half-tone process of illustration – opened new markets for photographers. At the end of the 1860s the Glasgow photographer Thomas Annan (1829-1887) made his now famous photographs of the slum areas of the city. These photographs are eloquent valedictions to the notorious way of living being swept away by progress and improvement. In the 1870s John Thomson (1837-1921), newly returned to London from his photographic exploration of China, made realistic tableaux of street workers, somewhat in the style of Dickens and Mayhew. However, these static and obviously arranged scenes were to be dramatically superseded by the candid-camera snapshots taken by Paul Martin twenty years later. With Martin (1864-1944) we find a recognizably twentieth-century figure. An artisan himself, he photographed as a man in the crowd – in the streets of London (almost in the street rather than on the pavement), on the beach at a holiday resort, among the crowds at a grand royal procession, or simply taking his pleasure on a day off in Battersea Park or on Hampstead Heath on a Sunday.

Simultaneously, photography became conscious of having a history, with heroic pioneers, with requirements of training, of aesthetic theory and austere artistic practice most trenchantly formulated by Dr Peter Henry Emerson (1856-1936). Emerson's photography describes with great skill the life and landscape of the Norfolk Broads – his equivalent (as an artist in the 1880s) of Brittany and Normandy. He prided himself on presenting his work with the care a 'painter-etcher' would bestow on an edition of engraved or etched prints, and he arranged for the destruction of negatives once the edition of prints (either platinum or, more commonly, photogravure) had been published. In 1890 Emerson called for the establishment of a major photographic institute complete with a first-rate library, well-fitted laboratories for chemistry and process work, a gallery for exhibitions, a print room for storing and studying prints, lecture rooms, darkrooms and 'a light refreshment bar, but no dinners, no billiards, nothing of any kind that will invite people to loaf and lounge about'. His colleague Frederick H. Evans (1853-1943) brought a similar, concentrated, austerity and delicacy to his practice in the same years, deriving inspiration from the Arts and Crafts Movement founded by William Morris. Their work provides the last monumental achievement of the nineteenth century in British photography and, in its style and seriousness, a prophecy of developments in the twentieth century.

Mark Haworth-Booth

1. William Henry Fox Talbot, *Bindweed*, c. 1839

2. William Henry Fox Talbot, *Books*,
photograph from *The Pencil of Nature*, 1844

3.   William Henry Fox Talbot, *Study of a Tree*, c. 1840-45

4. David Octavius Hill and Robert Adamson, *Hill and Johnston*, c. 1843-47

5. (Overleaf) Calvert Richard Jones, *The House of Sallust, Pompeii*, 1846

6. David Octavius Hill and Robert Adamson,
The Reverend Thomas Henshaw Jones, c. 1845

7.   David Octavius Hill and Robert Adamson,
Fisherman and Boys at Newhaven, c. 1843-47

8. David Octavius Hill and Robert Adamson,
The Birdcage, c. 1843-47

9. Roger Fenton, *The Long Walk, Windsor*, 1860

10. Roger Fenton, *Prince Leopold, Duke of Albany, Youngest Son of Queen Victoria*, 1854

11. Roger Fenton, *The British Museum, c.* 1860

12. Philip Henry Delamotte, *Preparing a Glass Case for Aquatic Animals during Construction of the Crystal Palace at Sydenham,* 1853

13. Benjamin Brecknell Turner, *Transept of the Crystal Palace, Hyde Park*, 1852

14. Comte de Montizon, *The Hippopotamus at the Zoological Gardens, Regent's Park, London*, 1855

15. Roger Fenton, *Cheddar Gorge*, 1858

16. John Dillwyn Llewelyn, *Bracken*, c. 1853-55

17. John Dillwyn Llewelyn, *Wales*, c. 1853-55

18. Roger Fenton, *The Bowder Stone, Borrowdale*, 1860

19. Francis Bedford, *Island of Philae, Egypt*, 1862

20. Oscar Gustav Rejlander, *Rejlander Presents the Volunteer Rejlander*, c. 1860

21. Oscar Gustav Rejlander, *The Two Ways of Life*, 1857

22. Henry Peach Robinson, *The Last Sigh*, 1858

23. George Washington Wilson, *Queen Victoria with John Brown*, 1863

24. Charles Clifford, *Fountain in Madrid*, early 1850s

25. Lady Hawarden, *Study from Life*, c. 1860

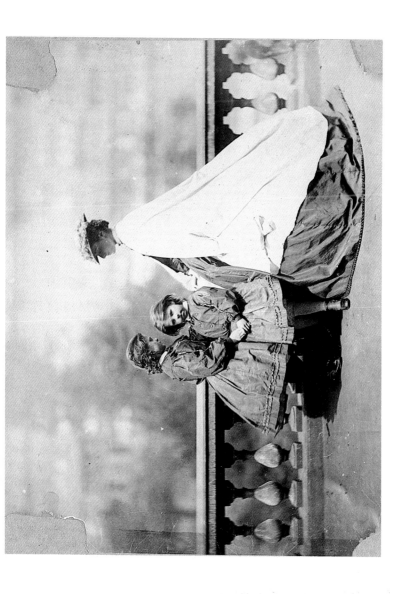

26. Robert Howlett, *Portrait of Isambard Kingdom Brunel*, 1857

27. Robert Howlett, *Construction of the* Great Eastern
in the Naval Dockyard at Millwall, 1857

28. Francis Frith, *The Colossus of Ramses II at Abu Simbel*, c. 1856-59

29. Francis Frith, *Pyramid of Dahshur, Egypt*, 1858

30. Frank Mason Good, *Abydos*, c. 1865

31. Julia Margaret Cameron, *Esme Howard*, 1869

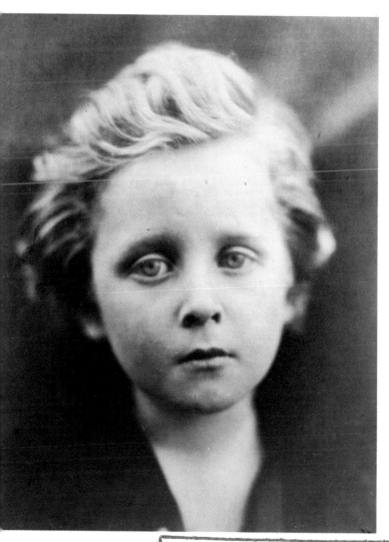

32. Julia Margaret Cameron, *The Kiss of Peace*, 1869

33. Julia Margaret Cameron, *Sir John Herschel*, 1867

34. Thomas Annan, *75 High Street, Glasgow*, 1868

35. Anonymous, *Portrait of Jane Morris*, 1865

36. Samuel Bourne, *Road Lined with Poplars, Kashmir*, c. 1865

Figure 50 a.

37. Samuel Bourne, *Salween River*, c. 1865

38. John Thomson, *The Temple of Nakon Wat, Cambodia*, c. 1864-65

J. Thomson

39. John Thomson, *Physic Street in Canton*, 1873

40. Lewis Carroll, *Xie Kitchin Reclining in a Garden Chair with a Japanese Umbrella*, c. 1875

41. Frank Meadow Sutcliffe, *Harbour View*, c. 1885

42. Frank Meadow Sutcliffe, *Stern Realities*, c. 1885

43. Frank Meadow Sutcliffe, *Natives of These Isles*, c. 1885

44. Frederick Hollyer, *Portrait of a Woman*, c. 1888

45. Peter Henry Emerson, photogravure from *Marsh Leaves*, 1890

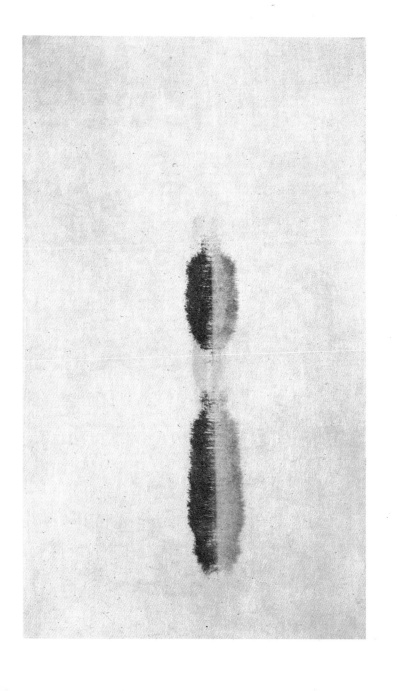

46. Peter Henry Emerson, *A Toad on the Path*, photograph from *Pictures of East Anglian Life*, 1888

47. Peter Henry Emerson, *The Poacher*, photograph from *Pictures of East Anglian Life*, 1888

48. Alfred Horsley Hinton, *Wild Landscape*, 1896

A. Horsley Hinton

49. Frederick Evans, *Aubrey Beardsley*, c. 1894

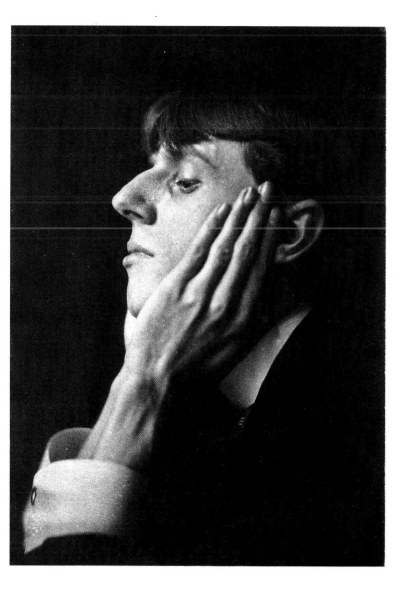

50. Anonymous, *Group Portrait*, c. 1895

51 and 52. Paul Martin, *Street Urchins*, c. 1885-1900, and *Victoria Park*, 1898

53. Frederick Evans, *Lincoln Cathedral, Stairway in the Southwest Tower*, 1898

54. Sir Benjamin Stone, *Westminster Abbey*, 1898

55. James Craig Annan, *Stirling Castle*, 1906

56. Herbert George Ponting, *The Castle Berg*, c. 1910-12

57. Oxley Grabham, *White Whale Killed in the River near York*, c. 1910

58. Archibald Cochrane, *The Trough*, 1908

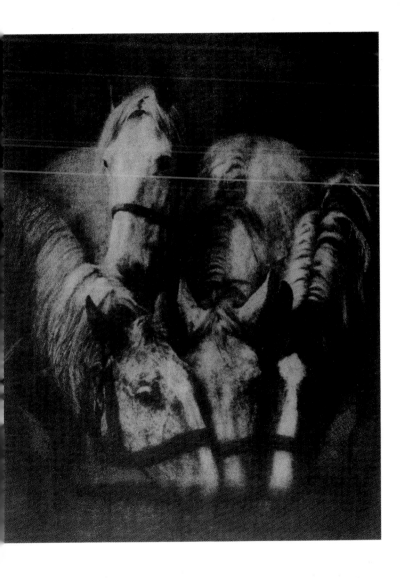

59. Francis J. Mortimer, *The Lifeboat*, early 1900s

60. J. Dudley Johnston, *Liverpool*, 1906

61. James McKissack, *Scarborough*, c. 1911

62. Alexander Keighley, *The Sphinx*, 1913

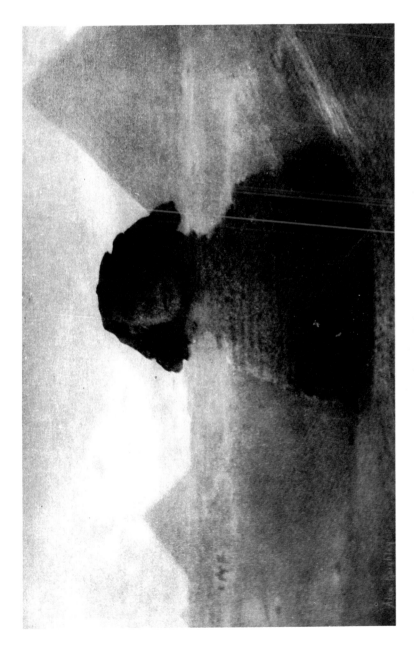

63. Rico Weber, *Rain*, 1913

BIOGRAPHIES

Bold figures in brackets refer to plate nos.

James Craig Annan (1864-1946). The second son of Thomas Annan, from whom he learnt photography, he studied photogravure with Klic in Vienna in 1883 and subsequently built up the reputation of the family firm in Glasgow, T. and R. Annan and Sons Ltd, suppliers of photographs and photogravures to the Queen. In around 1890 he began producing photogravures from Hill and Adamson's calotype negatives, thereby reviving public interest in their work. From 1894 he was an active member of the Linked Ring and sought to establish pictorial photography as a recognized art form on a level with the other arts **(55)**.

Thomas Annan (1829-1887). After training as an engraver, in 1855 he set up a photographic workshop in Glasgow, Thomas Annan Calotype Printers, concentrating in particular on photographing works of art. He also photographed landscapes and interiors, and in 1866 he was commissioned by the city council to do a series of photographs of the Glasgow slum areas. Published in 1900 under the title *The Old Closes and Streets of Glasgow*, this work was a landmark in the history of photography **(34)**.

Francis Bedford (1816-1894). An architect like his father, and a draughtsman and lithographer, he photographed the royal collections in 1854 and was later commissioned to photograph Prince Albert's native village in Bavaria. Bedford is known for his numerous views of Great Britain, and he also accompanied the Prince of Wales on his Grand Tour of the eastern Mediterranean in 1862. The photographic documentation of the trip has since been largely dispersed **(19)**.

Samuel Bourne (1834-1912). Bourne was a bank clerk before becoming a professional photographer in 1857. He spent the years 1863 to 1866 photographing various regions in India, in particular the Himalayas and Kashmir. He co-founded a photographic

workshop with Shepherd in Simla, and one in Calcutta in 1870. He also set up a cotton-manufacturing business, dividing his time between India and England **(36 and 37)**.

Julia Margaret Cameron (1815-1879). She was born into a comfortably off, cultured family in Calcutta and in 1838 married the diplomat Charles Hay Cameron. She moved to England in 1848 and in 1860 settled on the Isle of Wight. In 1863 she began to practise photography (producing collodion-on-glass negatives) and became friends with several prominent figures from the scientific and artistic worlds, including Watts, Tennyson and Herschel. Cameron regarded her photography as a creative act rather than a hobby and exhibited and sold her work. Skilful in the use of long exposure, soft focus, and atmospheric lighting effects, she specialized in portrait photographs and allegorical scenes inspired by the Bible or medieval legend. Her artistic style, bordering on painting, made her a precursor of pictorialism. She returned east to live in Ceylon in 1875 and died there four years later **(31, 32 and 33)**.

Lewis Carroll (1832-1898). The Reverend Charles Lutwidge Dodgson, author of *Alice's Adventures in Wonderland*, known by his literary pseudonym, Lewis Carroll, spent his entire life in Oxford, where he was a mathematics don and where he was ordained deacon in 1861. He discovered photography in 1856 and became a fervent protagonist of the art, confining his range to portraits and a few genre scenes. The only works he actually published were his portraits of fellow clergymen. His private work, discovered posthumously, was a paean to little girls, those occasional models he met through colleagues and friends in the years 1856 to 1880 **(cover and 40)**.

Charles Clifford (?-1863). He set up his studio in Madrid in 1852 and concentrated primarily on landscapes, views of monuments and historic sites in Spain, using the calotype and later the glass-negative process. Clifford was one of those English photographers who spent a great deal of time living as expatriates in the Mediterranean, and whose work was aimed at both the tourist and the art lover **(24)**.

Philip Henry Delamotte (1821-1889). The son of a painter, he was himself professor of drawing at King's College, Cambridge. At the end of the 1840s he was a calotypist and daguerreotypist and in 1855 he offered printing services and teaching courses using the collodion process. Delamotte's major work was a series of photographs (published in 1855) which he was commissioned to take of the reconstruction of the Crystal Palace at Sydenham in 1854. His photographs also illustrated a number of books, including *The Sunbeam* (1859) **(12)**.

Peter Henry Emerson (1856-1936). Born in Cuba, of an English mother, he moved to England with his family in 1869. He studied medicine at Cambridge and bought his first camera in 1881. In 1885 he visited the Norfolk Broads and co-founded the Camera Club of London. Influenced by the naturalist school of painting and by Impressionism, and convinced of the artistic status of photography, he expounded his views in various articles and papers, and in the book *Naturalistic Photography for Students of the Art* (1889). Emerson quickly came to recognize the limitations of photography, however, and abandoned his scientific theories, publishing, in 1891, *The Death of Naturalistic Photography*. His oeuvre – landscapes, peasants at work and scenes from daily life – survives in the form of platinotype and photogravure illustrations to seven books (1886-95) **(45, 46** and **47)**.

Frederick Henry Evans (1853-1943). Evans started out as a librarian in London before taking up photography, which he did for educational reasons. In the 1890s he undertook what can only be described as a campaign to capture in photographs the cathedrals of England and France, paying particular attention to the effects of lighting and perspective and adopting a rigorously disciplined

style. A technical purist who rejected the idea of retouching his photographs, he was elected a member of the Linked Ring, published in *Camera Work* and exhibited at Stieglitz's gallery (Gallery 291) in New York **(49** and **53)**.

Roger Fenton (1819-1869). Fenton studied law at the University of London before becoming a student of the painter Delaroche in Paris (1841-43). In 1844 he returned to London, abandoned his career as a painter and took up law again. It was at around this time that he became interested in photography. In 1852 he went to Russia and took photographs of Kiev, St Petersburg and Moscow. Photographer to the royal family and founder of The Photographic Society of London, he was nominated official photographer of the Crimean War in 1855. From 1856 to 1862 he concentrated on landscape and still life and took a special interest in English Gothic architecture **(9, 10, 11, 15** and **18)**.

Francis Frith (1822-1898). Born into a Quaker family, Frith started his working life in the grocery business (1845-55). In 1850 he opened a photographic studio in Liverpool. His trip to Egypt in 1856, from which he brought back numerous photographs of monuments, was a huge commercial success. In 1858 and 1859 he returned to Egypt and also went to Palestine and Syria, visiting the future tourist spots on the Grand Tour of the Middle East. Frith opened a photographic establishment in Reigate reproducing and selling his prints, and he published several photographically illustrated books, including a Bible (1862) **(28** and **29)**.

Frank Mason Good (active 1860s-1880s). One of the numerous photographers of Egypt and the Holy Land who followed in the wake of Francis Frith, he published stereoscopic views and illustrated a number of books **(30)**.

Lady Hawarden (1822-1865). Married to Viscount Hawarden, she took a large number of 'amateur' photographs inside her high-windowed London flat, using her children, her husband or her servants as models. Her 'Studies from Life' attracted critical attention when they were exhibited in 1863 and 1864 **(25)**.

David Octavius Hill (1802-1870) and **Robert Adamson** (1821-1848). These two artists have to be considered together, since their names are indissolubly linked on their photographic prints. Hill was a painter-lithographer in Edinburgh, co-founder and secretary of the Royal Scottish Academy in 1829, who became interested in photography in 1840. Commissioned in 1843 to paint a large commemorative composition of hundreds of ministers who had seceded from the Church of Scotland, Hill joined forces with Adamson and prepared his portraits from photographic models. Adamson had learnt the calotype process in 1842. Their collaboration led to the opening of a studio and continued up until 1847 with numerous portraits, landscapes and scenes of local life. Adamson died the following year (**4, 6, 7** and **8**).

Alfred Horsley Hinton (1863-1908). Following an art education, he worked in 1888 for a firm producing photographic materials and collaborated on the *Photographic Art Journal* (1888-91). A dedicated exponent of the pictorialist movement, he co-founded the Linked Ring in 1892 and contributed enthusiastically to the review *The Amateur Photographer*. English correspondent of the Photo Club de Paris, famous for his landscapes, Hinton preached an Impressionist approach that is illustrated by his book *L'Art photographique dans le paysage*, published in Paris in 1894 (**48**).

Frederick Hollyer (1837-1933). A pictorialist photographer who had affinities with the Pre-Raphaelite school, he became a member of the Linked Ring in 1893. His oeuvre includes many portraits of artists and writers, and reproductions of works of art (**44**).

Robert Howlett (1831-1858). An associate of Joseph Cundall, he produced portraits of Crimean War heroes, genre scenes and landscapes. His major work, however, was linked with the construction of the massive steamship the *Great Eastern*, a celebration of trade and technology (**26** and **27**).

J. Dudley Johnston (1868-1955). Johnston was a company director who took up photography as an amateur during a trip to Norway, but rapidly became an active member of various photographic associations and acted as a spokesman for the pictorialist aesthetic at the beginning of the 20th century. From 1923 to 1931 he was president of The Royal Photographic Society, one of his primary concerns being the setting up of collections (**60**).

Calvert Richard Jones (1804-1877). A mathematician, musician, painter and parson, educated at Oxford, Jones was introduced to photography by a cousin of William Henry Fox Talbot. In 1845 he went to Malta and Italy and returned from his travels with a collection of calotypes. He sold his prints through Fox Talbot and continued to travel and take photographs for another ten years or so. He was one of the first members of The Photographic Society of London (**5**).

Alexander Keighley (1861-1947). One of the 'great amateurs' of English photography, Keighley was much influenced by Henry Peach Robinson and chiefly concentrated on producing landscapes in an Impressionist style. A founder member of the Linked Ring, he continued the tradition of pictorialism well into the 20th century (**62**).

John Dillwyn Llewelyn (1810-1882). Llewelyn, who was married to a cousin of Fox Talbot, occupied a similar social and intellectual position to that of his relative, taking an interest in the various scientific and artistic questions of the day. He practised photography from 1839, but despite numerous studies and technical improvements, he remained an amateur. At the same time, however, his work displays a high level of technical skill (**16** and **17**).

Paul Martin (1864-1944). A Frenchman by origin, Martin emigrated to England with his family. In 1880 he became a wood engraver and found himself thus confronted with the problems involved in reproducing photographs in journals. He took advantage of the latest developments in the half-tone process and, armed with a disguised hand camera, set about supplying magazines with photographs of street scenes that seemed astonishingly natural. In 1896 he began experimenting with night photography, subsequently making a name for himself as one of the first photo-journalists (51 and 52).

Francis J. Mortimer (1874-1944). A journalist and illustrator, he was a member of the Linked Ring from its foundation in 1892. Mortimer's photographs are above all an expression of his overriding passion for the sea and capture the effects of waves and storms. Editor of *The Amateur Photographer* and *Photograms of the Year*, he played an important part in the diversification of photographic practices which led to the break-up of the Linked Ring, an association that was strictly pictorialist (59).

Herbert George Ponting (1871-1935). Ponting was one of those who took part in the California gold rush at the end of the 19th century. He photographed the Russo-Japanese War and was chosen by Captain Scott to accompany him as photographer on his expeditions to Antarctica in 1909 and 1910-11. Following these trips he gave a number of lectures, using his own photographs as illustrations (56).

Oscar Gustav Rejlander (1813-1875). This Swedish-born painter studied in Rome, then later moved to England, learning photography in 1853. He produced genre scenes and photographic portraits, discovering a method of printing a picture using several different negatives. The huge success of *The Two Ways of Life* in 1857 and Henry Peach Robinson's enthusiasm for this technique opened the way for competition between photography and painting and led on the one hand, through 'art photography', to pictorialism. Rejlander also photographed highly natural genre scenes that were close to snapshots in effect (20 and 21).

Henry Peach Robinson (1830-1901). A painter and draughtsman, with an interest in engraving, Robinson began taking photographs in 1852 and opened a studio in 1857. His success dates from 1858, the year in which he exhibited *Fading Away*, a photographic composition based on Rejlander's

technique of combining negatives. Robinson was the originator of the Brotherhood of the Linked Ring, formed in 1892, and after experimenting with landscapes and genre scenes he became an exponent of pictorialism and rural photography. His influence is largely bound up with his writings (comprising some ten books, including *Pictorial Effect in Photography*, 1869), which are known throughout Europe and in the United States and which preach an aesthetic not far from the rules of composition in painting (22).

Sir Benjamin Stone (1838-1914). Director of a glass factory in Birmingham, he began to take an interest in photography in 1888. His social and financial position enabled him to put together a work documenting English society that has since become a source of rather stolid images illustrating the end of the Victorian era (54).

Frank Meadow Sutcliffe (1853-1941). He took up photography in 1871, began collaborating with Francis Frith and in 1875 opened a studio in Whitby on the Yorkshire coast, where he spent his entire life. He felt little inclination to satisfy the popular demand for portraits, but found that his vocation lay, instead, in taking his camera out and about and capturing vignettes of fishermen at work, or children swimming, or certain effects created by the sky or the play of light. Influenced by Emerson, Sutcliffe was one of the principal adherents and theoreticians of photographic naturalism and a founder member of the Linked Ring (41, 42 and 43).

William Henry Fox Talbot (1800-1877). Fox Talbot studied science (with particular emphasis on mathematics and chemistry) at Cambridge. An intellectually curious man whose investigations brought him into contact with a whole range of disciplines, he developed the notion of fixing chemically the images of the camera lucida from which he made drawings during a trip to Italy in 1833. His first experiments with silver salts date from 1835. When, in 1839, the discovery of the daguerreotype was announced, Fox Talbot was obliged to disclose his own methods involving what he called 'photogenic drawings' (photographic impressions of plants on sensitized paper). He invented the calotype process, which used a 'negative' on paper by means of which a virtually limitless number of prints, also on paper, could be obtained. He brought photography to the attention of a much wider public when he opened his Reading print workshop in 1843 and published the first photographic album, *The Pencil of Nature*, in 1844. He set up another studio in London and was responsible for the invention of several photogravure processes. Fox Talbot's work, like that of all the pioneers of photography, is less well known today than it deserves (**1, 2** and **3**).

John Thomson (1837-1921). Best known as one of the first photographers to visit the Far East, which he did in 1862, Thomson set up a studio in Singapore and later one in Hong Kong. His *Illustrations of China and its People*, published in 1873-74 on his return to London, contains two hundred original photographs. Thomson went on to publish *Street Life in London* (1877-78), a series of street scenes documenting city life, later becoming official photographer to the Crown (**38** and **39**).

Benjamin Brecknell Turner (1815-1894). An amateur photographer, he familiarized himself with Fox Talbot's calotype process during the 1840s, becoming one of the most ardent exponents of this method for more than a decade, even when glass negatives had superseded the former technique. In the 1850s he produced numerous large-format rural landscapes that were rigorously classical in composition, and photographed ruins, trees and country lanes in a romantic style (**13**).

George Washington Wilson (1823-1893). A landscape painter who had done his training in Edinburgh, Wilson took up photography during the 1850s and became known principally for his instantaneous seascapes and stereoscopic views. He was Queen Victoria's photographer in Scotland and the author of a vast collection of landscapes and views documenting sites of Scottish interest, whose works can be found in numerous books on architecture and Scotland's historical and cultural heritage (**23**).

The Royal Photographic Society. When the Société Héliographique was founded in Paris in 1851, Roger Fenton studied its organization and it was following his proposals that The Photographic Society of London was founded, in 1853, by a group of amateur and scientific photographers. The society, which, under the patronage of Queen Victoria, became The Royal Photographic Society in 1894, was set up for the purposes of encouraging research into, and knowledge and practice of, the photographic art. Thanks to donations by its members, it has gathered together a collection of many thousands of photographs, mostly by British photographers, including representatives of pictorialism, which ranks as one of the most important in the world. In 1980 The Royal Photographic Society moved its premises and collections to Bath.

The Linked Ring. The Brotherhood of the Linked Ring was a photographic association, founded in London by Henry Peach Robinson and others in 1892, which broke with The Royal Photographic Society on the basis of a more strictly artistic approach to photography. The foundation of the Linked Ring marked the official beginning of pictorialism. It was followed by the formation of other breakaway groups in Europe and America, such as the Photo Club de Paris (1894) and New York's Photo-Secession (1902). The Linked Ring was rather an elite club, made up of co-opted members – something, in fact, of an artistic confraternity. Up until its dissolution in 1908 it continued to organize annual Salons, which were a developing ground for the pictorialist aesthetic, firmly placed by the group on an equal footing with the other arts.

PHOTO CREDITS

PHOTOFILE

Titles in this series include:
American Photographers of the Depression
Eugène Atget
Werner Bischof
The Origins of British Photography
Brassaï
Camera Work
Robert Capa
Henri Cartier-Bresson
Bruce Davidson
Robert Doisneau
Robert Frank
André Kertész
Jacques-Henri Lartigue
Photomontage
Marc Riboud
Man Ray
Duane Michals
Helmut Newton
The Nude
W. Eugene Smith
Weegee

The Photofile series is conceived and produced
by the Centre National de la Photographie, Paris,
under the direction of Robert Delpire.